EDWARD ALBEE has written and directed some of the greatest plays in contemporary American theater, three of which—*Three Tall Women*, *A Delicate Balance*, and *Seascape*—received Pulitzer Prizes. His most famous play, *Who's Afraid of Virginia Woolf?*, received the New York Drama Critics Circle Award for Best Play.

D0050364

Edward Albee

Three Tall Women

A PLAY IN TWO ACTS

A PLUME BOOK

PLUME
Published by the Penguin Group
Penguin Books USA Inc., 375 Hudson Street, New York, New York 10014, U.S.A.
Penguin Books Ltd, 27 Wrights Lane, London W8 5TZ, England
Penguin Books Australia Ltd, Ringwood, Victoria, Australia
Penguin Books Canada Ltd, 10 Alcorn Avenue, Toronto, Ontario, Canada M4V 3B2
Penguin Books (N.Z.) Ltd, 182–190 Wairau Road, Auckland 10, New Zealand

Penguin Books Ltd, Registered Offices: Harmondsworth, Middlesex, England

Published by Plume, an imprint of Dutton Signet, a division of
Penguin Books USA Inc. Previously published in a Dutton edition.

First Plume Printing, September, 1995
10 9 8 7 6 5 4 3 2 1

Three Tall Women first appeared, in its entirety, in *American Theatre* magazine.

 REGISTERED TRADEMARK—MARCA REGISTRADA

The Library of Congress has catalogued the Dutton edition as follows:

Albee, Edward
   Three tall women : a play in two acts / Edward Albee.
      p.   cm.
   ISBN: 0-525-93960-1 (hc.)
   ISBN: 0-452-27400-1 (pbk.)
   1. Aged women—Drama. 2. Mothers and sons—Drama. I. Title.
  PS3551.L25T48 1995   94–23234
  812'.54—dc20   CIP

Printed in the United States of America

Three Tall Women premiered at Vienna's English Theatre, Ltd, on June 14, 1991, produced by Franz Schafranek and American Producing Director, Glyn O'Malley. Edward Albee was the Director, Claire Cahill was Stage Manager and designed the set, with the following cast:

A	*Myra Carter*
B	*Kathleen Butler*
C	*Cynthia Bassham*
The Young Man	*Howard Nightingale*

The American premiere opened on July 30, 1992, at River Arts Repertory, Woodstock, New York, Lawrence Sacharow, Artistic Director and Director, with the following cast:

A	*Myra Carter*
B	*Marian Seldes*
C	*Jordan Baker*
The Young Man	*Michael Rhodes*

The set was designed by James Noone, costumes by Barbara Beccio, and lighting by Peter Waldron. Scott Glenn was Stage Manager.

The production of *Three Tall Women* with the same cast opened at the Vineyard Theatre in New York City on January 27, 1994: Douglas Aibel, Artistic Director; Jon Nakagawa, Managing Director. Muriel Stockdale designed the costumes; Phil Monat, lights. Elizabeth Berther was Production Stage Manager.

The production subsequently moved off Broadway to the Promenade Theatre where it was produced by Elizabeth I. McCann, Jeffrey Ash, and Daryl Roth. Brent Peek Productions served as General Manager; Roy Gabay, Company Manager; R. Wade Jackson, Production Stage Manager.

INTRODUCTION

People often ask me how long it takes me to write a play, and I tell them "all of my life." I know that's not the answer they're after—what they really want is some sense of the time between the first glimmer of the play in my mind and the writing down, and perhaps the duration of the writing down—but "all of my life" is the truest answer I can give, for it is the only one which is exact, since the thinking about the play and the putting it to paper vary so from play to play.

Few sensible authors are happy discussing the creative process—it is, after all, black magic, and may lose its power if we look that particular gift horse too closely in the mouth, or anywhere else, for that matter; further, since the creative process cannot be taught or learned, but only described, of what use is the discussion? Still, along with "where do your ideas come from?", the question is greatly on the mind of that tiny group of civilians who bother to worry it at all.

With *Three Tall Women* I can pinpoint the instant I began writing it, for it coincides with my first awareness of consciousness. I was in a group of four who were on a knoll (I could even now show you the exact spot, the exact knoll) observing the completion of a new house, the scaffolding still on it. There were three adults and tiny me—my adoptive mother, my adoptive father, my nanny (Nanny Church) and, in Nanny Church's arms—what? three-month-old Edward, certainly no older. My memory of the incident is wholly visual—the scaffolding, the people; and while I have no deep affection for it, it *is* my first awareness of being aware, and so I suppose I treasure it.

I have the kind of mind that does not retain much consciously—I experience, absorb, consider, banish into the deeps. Oh, should someone remind me of a significant event, its sights and sounds will come flooding back, but free of emotional baggage—that dealt with at the time of the incident, or catalogued elsewhere. And I know that my present self is shaped by as much self-deception as anyone else's, that my objectivities are guided by the maps I myself have drawn, and that nothing is really ever forgotten, merely filed away as inconvenient or insupportable.

So, when I decided to write what became *Three Tall Women*, I was more aware of what I did *not* want to do than exactly what I did want to accomplish. I knew my subject—my adoptive mother, whom I knew from my infancy (that knoll!) until her death over sixty years later, and who, perhaps, knew me as well. Perhaps.

I knew I did not want to write a revenge piece—could not honestly do so, for I felt no need for revenge. We had managed to make each other very unhappy over the years, but I was past all that, though I think she was not. I harbor no ill-will toward her; it is true I did not like her much, could not abide her prejudices, her loathings, her paranoias, but I did admire her pride, her sense of self. As she moved toward ninety, began rapidly failing both physically and mentally, I was touched by the survivor, the figure clinging to the wreckage only partly of her own making, refusing to go under.

No, it was not a revenge piece I was after, and I was not interested in "coming to terms" with my feelings toward her. I knew my feelings, I thought they were pretty much on the mark, and knew that I would not move much beyond the grudging respect I'd slowly developed for her. I was not seeking self-catharsis, in other words.

I realized then that what I wanted to do was write as objective a play as I could about a fictional character who resembled in every way, in every event, someone I had known very, very well. And it was only when I invented, when I translated fact intact into fiction, that I was aware I would be able to be accurate without prejudice, objective without the distortive folly of "interpretation."

I did not cry and gnash my teeth as I put this woman down on paper. I cannot recall suffering either *with* her or because of her as I wrote her. I recall being very interested in what I was doing—fascinated by the horror and sadness I was (re)creating.

Writers have the schizophrenic ability to both participate in their lives and, at the same time, observe themselves participating in their lives. Well . . . some of us have this ability, and I suspect it was this (frightening?) talent that allowed me to write *Three Tall Women* without prejudice, if you will.

I know that I "got her out of my system" by writing this play, but then again I get *all* the characters in *all* of my plays out of my system by writing about them.

Finally, when I based the character "Grandma" (*The American Dream, The Sandbox*) on my own (adoptive) maternal grandmother, I noticed that while I liked the lady a lot—we were in alliance against those folk in the middle—the character I created was both funnier and more interesting than the model. Have I done that here? Is the woman I wrote in *Three Tall Women* more human, more multifaceted than its source? Very few people who met my adoptive mother in the last twenty years of her life could abide her, while many people who have seen my play find her fascinating. Heavens, what have I done?!

Edward Albee
Montauk, NY
1994

CHARACTERS

A   a very old woman; thin, autocratic, proud, as together as the ravages of time will allow. Nails scarlet, hair nicely done, wears makeup. Lovely nightgown and dressing gown.

B   looks rather as A would have at 52; plainly dressed.

C   looks rather as B would have at 26.

THE BOY   23 or so; preppy dress (jacket, tie, shirt, jeans, loafers, etc.)

THE SETTING

The play is set in a "wealthy" bedroom, French in feeling. Pastels, with blue predominant. A bed upstage center, with a small bench at its foot. Lacy pillows, a lovely spread. Nineteenth century French paintings. Two light armchairs, beautifully covered in silk. If there is a window, silk swags. Pastel carpeted floor. Two doors, one to left, one to right. Archways for both.

Note: Act Two has the same set as Act One, except for medical stuff to be decided.

ACT ONE

At rise, A is in the stage left armchair, B in the stage right one, C on the bed foot bench.

It is afternoon.

(*Some silence.*)

A

(*An announcement from nowhere; to no one in particular.*)
I'm ninety-one.

B

(*Pause.*) Is that so?

A

(*Pause.*) Yes.

C

(*Small smile.*) You're ninety-*two*.

A

(*Longer pause; none too pleasant.*) Be that as it *may*.

B

(*To* C.) Is that so?

C

(*Shrugs; indicates papers.*) Says so here.

B

(*Pause; stretching.*) Well . . . what does it matter?

C

Vanity is amazing.

B

So's forgetting.

A

(*General.*) I'm ninety-one.

B

(*Accepting sigh.*) OK.

C

(*Smaller smile.*) You're ninety-*two*.

B

(*Unconcerned.*) Oh . . . let it alone.

C

No! It's important. Getting things . . .

B

It doesn't matter!

C

(*Sotto voce.*) It does to *me*.

A

(*Pause.*) I know because he says, "You're exactly thirty
years older than I am; I know how old I am because I
know how old *you* are, and if you ever forget how old
you are ask me how old *I* am, and then you'll know."
(*Pause.*) Oh, he's said that a lot.

C

What if he's wrong?

A

(*From a distance; curiously lighter, higher voice.*) What?

B

Let it *be*.

C

(*Still to* A.) What if he's wrong? What if he's not thirty
years younger than you?

A

(*Oddly loud, tough.*) You'd think he'd know how old he
is!

C

No, I mean . . . what if he's wrong about how old *you*
are.

A

(*Pause.*) Don't be silly. How couldn't he be thirty years
younger than me when I'm thirty years older than he
is? He's said it over and over. (*Pause.*) Every time he
comes to see me. What is today?

B

It's (*whatever day it is in reality*).

A

You see?!

C

(*A bit as if to a child.*) Well, one of you might be wrong,
and it might not be him.

B

(*Small sneer.*) *He.*

C

(*Quick smile.*) Yes; I know.

A

Don't be stupid. *What* is it? *What day* is it?

B

It's (*ibid.*).

A

(*Shakes her head.*) No.

C

(*Interested.*) No what?

A

No it *isn't*.

B

OK.

C

(*To* A.) What day do you *think* it is?

A

(*Confusion.*) What day is it? What day do I . . . ? (*Eyes narrowing.*) Why, it's today, of course. What day do you *think* it is?! (*Turns to* B*; cackles.*)

B

Right on, girl!

C

(*Scoffs.*) What an answer! What a dumb . . .

A

Don't you talk to me that way!

C

(*Offended.*) Well! I'm sorry!

A

I pay you, don't I? You can't talk to me that way.

C

In a way.

A

(*A daring tone.*) What?!

C

Indirectly. You pay someone who pays me, someone who . . .

A

Well; there; you see? You can't talk to me that way.

B

She isn't talking to you that way.

A

What?

B

She isn't *talking* to you that way.

A

(*Dismissive laugh.*) I don't know what you're talking about. (*Pause.*) Besides.

(*Silence; then she cries. They let her. It begins in self-pity, proceeds to crying for crying's sake, and concludes with rage and self-loathing at having to cry. It takes quite a while.*)

B

(*When it's over.*) There. Feel better?

C

(*Under her breath.*) Honestly.

B

(*To* A.) A good cry lets it all out.

A

(*Laughs; sly.*) What does a *bad* one do? (*Laughs again;* B *joins her.*)

C

(*Shakes her head in admiration.*) Sometimes you're so . . .

A

(*Ugly; suddenly.*) What?!

C

(*Tiny pause.*) Never *mind.* I was going to say something *nice.* Never *mind.*

A

(*To* B.) What did she say?! She mumbles all the time.

C

I don't mumble! (*Annoyance at herself.*) Never mind!

A

How is anybody expected to hear what she says?!

B

(*Placating.*) She didn't finish her sentence. It doesn't matter.

A

(*Small, smug triumph.*) I'll *bet* it doesn't.

C

(*Dogged, but not unpleasant.*) What I meant was you may have been incorrect about your age for so long—may have made up the fiction so many years ago, though why anyone would lie about one year . . .

B

(*Weary.*) Let her alone; let her have it if she wants to.

C

I will *not*.

A

Have what?!

C

Why you would lie about one *year*? I can imagine taking off ten—or *trying* to. Though more probably seven, or five—good and tricky—but *one*?! Taking off *one year*? What kind of vanity is *that*?

B

(*Clucks.*) How you go *on*.

A

(*Imitation.*) How you go *on*.

C

(*Purrs.*) How I go on. So, I can understand ten, or five, or seven, but not one.

B

How you *do*.

A

(*To* C.) How you *do*. (*To* B.) How *what*?!

B

How she goes on.

A

(*Cheerful.*) Yes! How you go *on*!

C

(*Smiles.*) Yes; I do.

A

(*Suddenly, but not urgently.*) I want to go.

C

On?

A

(*More urgently.*) I want to go. I want to go.

B

You want to go? (*Rises.*) You want the pan? Is it number
one? Do you want the pan?

A

(*Embarrassed to discuss it.*) No . . . Noooo!

B

Ah. (*Moves to* A.) All right. Can you walk?

A

(*Weepy.*) I don't know!

B

Well, we'll try you. OK? (*Indicates walker.*) You want the
walker?

A

(*Near tears.*) I want to walk! I don't know! Anything! I
have to *go*! (*Starts to fret-weep.*)

B

All right! (*She moves* A *to a standing position. We discover*
A*'s left arm is in a sling, useless.*)

A

You're hurting me!! You're hurting me!!

B

All right; I'm being careful!

A

No, you're *not*!!

B

Yes, I am!

A

No, you're *not*!!!

B

(*Angry.*) Yes, I *am.*

A

No, you're *not*! (*On her feet, weeping, shuffling with* B*'s help, off.*) You're trying to hurt me; you know how I hurt!!

B

(*To* C, *as they exit.*) Hold the fort.

C

I will. I will hold the fort. (*Muffled exchanges offstage.* C *looks toward them, shakes her head, looks back down.*)

(*Both to herself and to be heard.*) I suppose one could lie about one year—some kind of one-upmanship, a private vengeance, perhaps, some tiny victory, maybe. (*Shrugs.*) I don't know, maybe these things get important. Why can't I be nice?

B

(*Reenters.*) Made it that time. (*Sighs.*) And so it goes.

C

Not always, eh?

B

In the morning, when she wakes up she wets—a kind
of greeting to the day, I suppose: the sphincter and the
cortex not in sync. Never during the *night*, but *as* she
wakes.

C

Good morning to the morning, eh?

B

Something to something.

C

Put a diaper on her.

B

(*Shakes her head.*) She won't have it. I'm working on it,
but she won't have it.

C

Rubber sheet?

B

Won't have it. Get her up, put her in the chair and she
does the other. Give her a cup of coffee . . .

C

Black.

B

(*Chuckles.*) Half cream and all that sugar! Three
spoons! How has she lived this long? Give her a cup of
coffee, put her in her chair, give her a cup of coffee,
and place your bets.

C

(*Looks at the chair she is in.*) *What* chair?! *This* chair?!

B

(*Laughs.*) You got it. Don't worry.

C

It must be awful.

B

(*Deprecating.*) *For whom?*

C

(*Rising to it.*) For her! You're paid. It's probably awful for you, too, but you're paid.

B

As she never ceases to inform me . . . *and* you.

C

To begin to lose it, I mean—the control, the loss of dignity, the . . .

B

Oh, stop it! It's downhill from sixteen on! For all of us!

C

Yes, but . . .

B

What *are* you, *twenty* something? Haven't you figured it out yet? (*Demonstrates.*) You take the breath in . . . you let it out. The first one you take in you're upside down and they slap you into it. The last one . . . well, the last one you let it all out . . . and that's it. You start . . . and then you stop. Don't be so soft. I'd like to see children learn it—have a six-year-old say, I'm dying and know what it means.

C

You're horrible!

B

Start in young; make 'em aware they've got only a little time. Make 'em aware they're dying from the minute they're alive.

C

Awful!

B

Grow up! Do *you* know it? Do *you* know you're dying?

C

Well, of course, but . . .

B

(*Ending it.*) Grow up.

A

(*Wobbling, shuffling in.*) A person could die in there and nobody'd care.

B

(*Bright.*) Done already!

A

A person could die! A person could fall down and break something! A person could die! Nobody would care!

B

(*Going to her.*) Let me help you.

A

(*Good arm flailing.*) Get your *hands* off me! A person could die for all anybody'd care.

C

(*To herself, but to be overheard.*) Who is this . . . person?
A person could do this, a person could do . . .

B

It's a figure of speech.

C

(*Mildly sarcastic.*) No. Really?

B

(*Not rising to it.*) So they tell me.

A

(*Flailing about.*) Hold *on* to me! Do you want me to
fall?! You want me to *fall*!

B

Yes, I want you to fall; I want you to fall and shatter
in . . . ten pieces.

C

Or five, or seven.

A

Where's my chair? (*Sees it perfectly well.*) Where's my
chair gone to?

B

(*Playing the game.*) Goodness, where's her chair *gone*
to?! Somebody's taken her *chair*!

C

(*Realizing.*) What?!

A

(*Does she know? Probably.*) Who's got my chair?

C

(*High horse.*) I'm sorry! (*Gets up quickly; moves away.*)
Your majesty!

B

(*Placating.*) There's your chair. Do you want your pillow? Shall I get you your pillow? (*To* C.) Fetch her
pillow.

A

I want to sit *down*.

B

Yes, yes. Here we go. (*Gently lowers* A *into the vacated
armchair.*)

C

(*At bed.*) Which *pillow?*

B

(*To* A.) Are you comfortable? Do you want your pillow?

A

(*Petulant.*) Of *course* I'm not comfortable; of *course* I
want my pillow.

C

(*At the bed still; to* B.) I don't know which one!

B

(*Moving to the bed.*) It's two, actually, one for the back
(*Takes it.*) and this one for the arm. (*Takes it; moves
toward* A.) Here we are; lean forward. (*Positions back pillow.*) That's a girl.

A

My arm! My arm! Where's the pillow?!

B

Here we go. (*Arranges arm pillow.*) All comfy? (*Silence.*)
All comfy?

A

What?

B

Nothing. (*A knowing smile to* C.)

C

And so it goes?

B

Uh-huh.

C

What a production.

B

You haven't see anything.

C

I bet!

A

(*To* B.) You can't just leave me in there like that. What
if I fell? What if I died?

B

(*Considers it; calm.*) Well . . . if you fell I'd either hear
you or you'd raise a racket, and if you died what would
it matter?

A

(*Pause; then she laughs; true enjoyment.*) You can say that
again! (*Is amused at seeing* C *not amused.*) What's the
matter with you?

C

(*Small silence, until she realizes she's being talked to.*) Who?!
Me?!

A

Yes. You.

C

What's the *matter* with me?

B

(*Amused.*) That's what she *said.*

A

That's what I *said.*

C

(*Panicking a little.*) What are you all doing—ganging up
on me?

B

(*To* A.) Is that what we're doing?

A

(*Enjoying it greatly.*) May be!

C

(*To defend herself.*) There's *nothing* the matter with me.

B

(*Sour smile.*) Well . . . you just *wait.*

Λ

What did she say?

B

She says there's nothing the matter with her—Miss Perfect over there.

C

I didn't *say* that; that's not what I . . . !!

A

(*To* B; *sincere.*) Why is she *yelling* at me?!

B

She's *not.*

C

I'm *not*!

B

Now you are.

A

You see?! (*Confused.*) What day is it?

B

It's (*whatever day it is in reality*).

A

Will he come today? Is today the day he comes?

B

No; not today.

A

(*Whining.*) Why not?!

B

(*Making nothing of it.*) Oh, he probably has something else to do; he probably has a full schedule.

A

(*Teary.*) He never comes to see me, and when he does he never stays. (*A sudden shift in tone to hatred.*) *I'll* fix him; I'll fix *all* of 'em. They all think they can treat me

like this. You all think you can get away with anything.
I'll fix you all.

C

(*To* B, *an aside.*) Is it always like this?

B

(*Overly patient.*) No . . . it's often very pleasant.

C

Huh!

A

(*Muttering now.*) You all want something; there's nobody doesn't want something. My mother taught me
that; be careful, she said; they all want something; she
taught me what to expect, me and my sister. She pre-
pared us and somebody had to. I mean, we were girls
and that was way back then, and it was different then.
We didn't have a lot, and being a girl wasn't easy. We
knew we'd have to make our own way, and being a girl
back then . . . why am I talking about this?!

B

Because you want to.

A

That's right. She tried to prepare us . . . for going out
in the world, for men, for making our own way. Sis
couldn't do it; that's too bad. *I* could; *I* did. I met him
at a party, and he said he'd seen me before. He'd been
married twice—the first one was a whore, the second
one was a drunk. He was funny! He said, Let's go riding in the park, and I said all right . . . scared to death.
I lied; I said I rode. *He* didn't care; he wanted me; I
could tell that. It only took six weeks.

B

Good girl!

A

We had horses when we were married; we had a stable; we had saddle horses; we rode.

C

(*Mildly.*) Hoity-toity.

A

I learned to ride and I was very good.

B

(*Encouraging.*) I'm sure!

C

(*Mildly contemptuous.*) *How* are you sure?!

B

Shhhhhhh.

A

(*Childlike enthusiasm.*) I rode sidesaddle and I rode astride, and I drove ponies—hackneys—and I loved it all. He would go with me and we would ride every morning, and the dalmatian would go with us—what was her name . . . Suzie? No. We had good horses and we showed them and we won all the ribbons, and we kept them in a big case down in the . . . no, that was the other house. We kept them. (*Pause; reinvigorating herself.*) And cups. All the silver cups we won, and bowls, and platters. We knew all the judges but that's not why we would win: we won because we were the best.

C

(*Under her breath.*) Of course.

B

(*Sotto voce.*) Be decent.

A

(*Dismissive.*) Oh, she'll learn. (*Back to the memory.*) We had horses! I knew all the judges, and I'd go in the ring when we were in the championships, and I'd sit there and I'd watch the horses—I never rode when we were in the championships; Earl did that; he was our rider. I would sit there and watch with the judges. They all knew me; we were famous; we had a famous stable, and when the judging was done they'd tell me if we'd won, and we almost always did, and if they told me, and they almost always did, I'd signal. I'd take my hat off and I'd touch my hair (*Does it: touches hair.*) and that way they'd know we'd won.

C

(*To* B; *whispers.*) Who?!

(B *shrugs, keeps her eyes on* A.)

A

(*Very rational; explaining.*) Everyone in our box. (*Childish again.*) Oh, I used to love it, riding in the morning, going to the stable in the station wagon in my coat and jodhpurs and my derby, and petting . . . what was her name?, the dalmatian—Suzie, I think . . . no—and mounting and riding off. Sometimes he came with me and sometimes he didn't. Sometimes I went off alone.

C

(*To* B.) Who?

B

Her husband, most likely. (*To* A.) Did you ride when you were little?

A

(*A little, deprecating laugh.*) No. We were poor.

C

(*To* A.) Poor? Really . . . poor?

A

Well, no; not really poor; my father was an architect;
he designed furniture; he made it.

C

That's not an architect, that's . . .

B

Let it be.

A

He made such beautiful furniture; he was an architect.
Strict, but fair. No, my *mother* was strict. No, they were
both strict. *And* fair. (*This confuses her; she cries.*)

B

Now, now.

A

I don't know what I'm saying! What am I *saying*?

B

(*Comforting.*) You're talking about horses; you were
talking about riding, and we asked: when you were a
little girl . . .

A

(*Rational; tough.*) We never rode; the neighbors had a
horse but we never rode it. I don't think my sister ever
rode. But I can't swim. (*Conspiratorial whisper.*) She
drank.

C

When she was a little girl?

B

Oh, please!

A

(*Truly innocent.*) What? What are we talking about?

B

Horses. You didn't ride when you were a little girl.

A

You rode if you were a farmer or if you were rich.

C

(*Mildly mocking.*) Or if you were a rich *farmer*.

B

Shhhhhhh.

A

(*Of* C, *to* B.) She'll learn. (*To* C; *ominous.*) Won't you.

C

(*Flustered laugh.*) Well, I dare *say*.

A

(*Story again.*) I wasn't rich until I got married, and I wasn't really right then 'til later. It all adds up. We had saddle horses; we rode. I learned to ride and I was very good. I rode sidesaddle and I rode astride, and I drove ponies—hackneys . . .

C

. . . and you loved it all.

B

Shhhhhhh.

A

And I what?

C

You loved it all.

B

You loved it all.

A

I did?

B

So you say.

A

(*Laughs.*) Well, then, it must be true. I didn't like sex much, but I had an affair.

C

(*Interested.*) Oh?

A

(*Suddenly suspicious.*) What?! What do you want!?

B

She doesn't want anything.

A

(*Off again.*) We used to ride. *He* would go with me— not all the time. Sometimes I would go off alone, or with the dog, part way, never too far from the stable; she had a cat she was in love with. She'd go back, but I'd go on. I had my jodhpurs and my coat and my switch and my derby hat. I always rode in all my cos-

tume. Never go out except you're properly dressed,
I always say. I'd drive the station wagon from the
house—I loved to drive. I was good at it. I was good at
everything; I *had* to be; *he* wasn't. I'd drive in the
station wagon to the stable, and Earl would be there,
or . . . or one of the stable boys: Tom . . . or Bradley.
(*Long pause.*) Am I doing in my panties?! (*Starts to cry.*)

B

(*Leisurely.*) Well . . . let's see. (*Goes to* A.) Upseedaisy!
(*Raises her; she whimpers; cries more.* B *feels under* A.) Nope,
but I bet you're going to. Off you go. (*Helps* A *off.*)

C

Hold the fort?

(*Goes to window; looks out; looks at bed; goes to it; smooths
the covers.* B *reenters.*) Why am I doing this?

B

Because it's unnecessary? Because I've already done it?

C

The princess and the pea, maybe? What's wrong with
her arm?

B

She fell and broke it. It didn't heal. Mostly they don't
at that age. They put pins in it, metal pins; the bone
disintegrates around the pins and the arm just hangs
there. They want to take it off.

C

What?!

B

(*Matter of fact.*) The arm; they want to take the *arm* off.

C

(*Protest*.) No!

B

(*Shrugs*.) It hurts.

C

Still!

B

She won't *let* them.

C

I shouldn't *think* so.

B

What do *you* know? She makes us go into the city once
a week—to see the surgeon, the one who set it, the
one who wants to take it off. God, he's almost as old
as she is! She trusts him, she says. She goes in once a
week, and she makes them x-ray it, and *look* at it, and
each time the pins are looser, and the bone is gone
more, and she tells the old guy—the surgeon—it's so
much better, and she wants him to agree, and he waf-
fles, and he looks at me and I'm no help, and she
makes him promise that he'll never take the arm off,
and won't let anyone *else* do it either, and he prom-
ises—assuming she'll forget? Probably; but she won't.
There are some things she never forgets. He promised
me; you were there; you heard him. I think she says
that every other day: He promised me; you were there;
you heard him.

(*A crack of glass from offstage.*)
Oh, God!

(*She exits. From offstage now.*) Now, why did you do that?!
You naughty, naughty girl! Bad, bad girl! (A *hoots and*

cackles offstage.) What do I have to do—take everything away from you? Huh?!

(A *appears onstage again, hooting and giggling, followed by* B.)

A

(*Drifting, hobbling; very happy; to* C.) I broke the glass! I took the glass and I threw it down in the sink! I broke the glass and now she has to clean it up!

(B *has reentered.*)

B

Bad girl!

A

I broke the glass! I broke the glass!

(*Giggles; suddenly her face collapses and she cries; then:*) I have to sit down! I can't sit down by my*self*! Why won't somebody help me?!

B

(*Helping her.*) Now, now; here we go.

A

Ow! Ow!

B

All right, now.

C

(*Under her breath.*) Jesus!

B

(*To* C; *settling* A.) *You're* a big help.

C

(*Cold.*) I didn't know I was supposed to be.

B

(*Sneers.*) Just here from the lawyer, eh?

C

Yes; just here from the lawyer.

A

(*Suddenly suspiciously alert.*) What? What did you say?

B

(*Matter of fact.*) I said—well, what I implied was, since she's here from the lawyer, why should she behave like a human being; why should she be any help; why should she . . .

A

(*To* C; *happy.*) You're from Harry?

C

No; Harry's dead; Harry's been dead for years.

A

(*Tears again.*) Harry's *dead*? When did *Harry* die?

C

(*Loud.*) Thirty years ago!

A

(*Tiny pause; tears off.*) Well, *I* knew *that*. What are you talking about *Harry* for?

C

You asked if I'd come from Harry; you asked . . .

                              A

I wouldn't do anything that *stupid.*

                              B

(*Amused; to* C.) And so it goes.

                              A

(*Clarifying it for the world.*) Harry *used* to be my lawyer,
but that was *years* ago. Harry died—what? Thirty years
ago?—Harry died. Now his son's the lawyer. I go to
him; well, he comes to me; *some*times I go to him.

                              C

Yes; you do. *And* yes he does.

                              A

Why are *you* here?

                              C

(*Sighs.*) Some things have been . . . misplaced; aren't
being done. Some things . . .

                              A

(*Panic.*) Somebody's stealing things?!

                              C

No no no no. We send you papers to sign and you
don't sign them; we call you and you don't call back;
we send you checks to sign and you don't sign them;
things like that.

                              A

I don't know what you're talking about.

                              C

Well . . .

A

None of it's true! You're lying! Get Harry on the
phone!

C

Harry is . . .

B

(*To* A.) Excuse me? The "I'll get to it" pile?

A

(*Suspicious of* B now.) What?!

B

(*Calm.*) The "I'll get to it" pile?

A

I don't know *what* you're talking about.

C

(*To* B.) Papers? Checks?

B

(*Broad.*) Oh . . . lots of stuff.

A

(*Adamant.*) There's *nothing*!

C

(*To* B.) What *is* there? What *is* it?

B

(*To* A; *patiently.*) You have a drawer full; the bills come
and you look at them, and some of them you send on
and they get paid, and some of them you say you can't
remember and so you don't send them, and . . .

A

(*Defiant.*) Why would I send in a bill for something I never ordered?

B

(*Shuts eyes briefly.*) And they send you your checks—to sign? To pay bills? And some of them you sign because you remember what they were for, but some of them—some of the checks—you can't remember?

A

I *what?*!

B

(*Smiles tolerantly.*) . . . you don't remember what they're for and so you don't sign them and you put them in the drawer.

A

So?

B

(*Shrugs.*) These things pile up.

C

I *see*; I *see*.

A

Everybody out there's ready to rob me blind. I'm not made of money, you know.

B

(*Laughs.*) Yes, you *are*. (*To* C.) Isn't she?

C

(*Smiles.*) More or less.

A

(*Conspiratorially.*) They'd steal you blind if you didn't pay attention: the help, the stores, the markets, that little Jew makes my furs—what's her name? She's nice. They all rob you blind if you so much as turn your back on them. All of them!

C

We've asked you: let all your bills come to us; we'll know what to do; let me *bring* you your checks every month; I'll stay here while you sign them. Whatever you like.

A

(*A superior smile, but hesitant around the edges.*) None of you think I can handle my own affairs? I've done it for . . . when he was so sick I did it all; I did all the bills; I did all the checks; I did everything.

C

(*Gentle.*) But now you don't *have* to.

A

(*Proud.*) I didn't have to then: I *wanted* to. I wanted everything to be *right*; and I do now; I still do!

C

Well, of *course* you do.

B

Of *course* you do.

A

(*Ending it; superior.*) And so I'll handle my own affairs, thank you.

C

(*Defeated; shrugs.*) Well; certainly.

B

And *I'll* watch you *pretend* to handle them.

A

And I watch you, every one of you. I used to love horses.

B

It's just people you don't like.

A

(*Noncommittal.*) Oh? Is that it? We rode western saddle, too. It was when he almost died—the first time, the first time I was with him. He had a blood infection. He was hunting, they were all hunting, and a gun went off and it hit him in the arm, the shoulder.

(*Touches hers; realizes the parallel; smiles sadly.*) My God! (*Pause.*) They shot him in the shoulder, and they didn't get all the bullet out, and it got infected and his arm swelled up like a balloon and they lanced it and it burst and there was pus all over . . .

C

Stop!

B

(*Cold.*) Why? What's it to you?

(C *shudders.*)

A

. . . and they put drains in it and there weren't any medicines then . . .

B

No antibiotics, you mean.

A

What?

B

No antibiotics.

A

Yes, and it wouldn't go away and it would get worse,
and everybody said he was going to die, but I wouldn't
let him! I said, No! he is not going to die! I told that
to the doctors, and I told him that, too, and he said
all right, he would try, if I would sleep with him, if I
wouldn't leave him alone at night, be next to him, and
I did and it smelled so awful—the pus, the rot, the . . .

C

Don't! Please!

A

. . . and they said take him to the desert, bake his arm
in the hot sun, and so we went there—we went to
Arizona—and he sat in the baking sun all day—his arm
oozing, and stinking, and splitting and . . . and in six
months it went away and the arm went down in size
and there was no more pus and he was saved—except
for the scars, all the scars, and I learned to ride western
saddle.

B

My, my.

A

And it was outside of Phoenix—Camelback Mountain;
we used to ride out into the desert. And the movie star
was there—the one who married the young fellow who
ran the studio; she had eyes of a different color.

C

(*Small pause.*) She had *what?*

A

She had eyes of a different color: one eye was blue, or
something, and the other one was green, I think.

C

(*To* B.) Who *was* this?

(B *shrugs.*)

A

Oh, she was a big star; she was tiny and she had a very
big head. I think *she* drank too.

B

You think *everyone* drinks. Merle Oberon?

A

No; of course not! *You* know!

B

(*Enjoying this a little.*) How long ago *was* this? Claire
Trevor?

A

Oh . . . when I was there; when we were there. She was
tiny! She had two eyes!

B

In the thirties?

A

Probably. She had a son; she cooked an egg on the
sidewalk; it was so hot. He *told* me.

C

(*Lost.*) Her . . . son . . . told you?

A

No! Ours! He was a little boy, too; he played with all
the other children: the chewing gum twins; *that* one.

B

That must have been before the *war.*

C

Which one?!

B

Civil.

A

(*Triumphant.*) Thalberg! *That's* who she married. Ar-
nold Thalberg; he was a real smart little Jew.

B

(*To* C; *ironic.*) All smart Jews are *little.* Have you noticed? (*To* A.) Irving; *Irving* Thalberg.

C

(*Cold.*) I'm a Democrat; I notice a lot of things.

B

Most of us *are*; most of us *do.* But still, it's fascinating,
isn't it—grisly, but fascinating. She doesn't *mean* anything by it—or if she did, once, she doesn't now. It just
falls out.

A

(*Joyous.*) Norma Shearer!

B

Of course!

C

Who?

A

(*Laughs.*) What's the matter with all you people?!

C

(*Explaining.*) We're Democrats.

A

What?

C

Well, you asked what the matter was.

A

Don't you get fresh!

B

My God! I haven't heard that in a long time. (*Imitates.*)
Don't you get fresh!

A

My mother would say that to me all the time: Don't
you get fresh! To Sis and me. She made us eat everything she put before us, and wash the dishes; she made
us know what being a grown-up was. She was strict but
fair. No, that was our father; no, that was both of them.
(*A little girl whine.*) They're dead; Sis, they're dead!

C

A smart little Jew?

B

At least she didn't say kike.

A

(*Back to her memory.*) She would make us write thank-
you notes, and take little gifts whenever we went some-

where, and made us wash everything we wore the night
we wore it, by hand, before we went to bed. Sometimes
Sis wouldn't and I had to do hers, too. She made us
be proper young ladies.

C

And go to church twice a day? And pray a lot?

A

What? Oh, yes, we went to church but we didn't talk
about it very much. We took it for granted, I suppose.
(*To* B.) How much did you *steal*?

B

(*Not rising to it.*) When?

A

Whenever.

B

(*Drawling.*) Well, I waited until you were asleep . . .

A

I never sleep.

B

. . . until you were pretending to be asleep, and then
I went into the silver closet and took down all the big
silver bowls, and I stuck them up under my skirt, and
I waddled out into the hall . . .

A

Joke about it if you want to. (*A sudden fit of giggles.*) You
must have looked *funny*!

B

(*Playing along.*) Well, I suppose.

A

Waddling out like that; you probably clanked, too.

B

Yes; I'm sure I did. Clank, clank.

A

(*Hoots.*) Clank, clank!

(*Notices* C *isn't amused; tough.*) You don't think *any*-thing's funny, do you?

C

Oh, yes; I'm just trying to decide what I think's really the most hilarious—unpaid bills, anti-Semitism, senil-ity, or . . .

B

Now, now. Play in your own league, huh?

C

(*Miffed.*) Well! I'm *sorry*!

A

(*Looks right at* C.) I'll have to talk to Harry about you.

B

(*Ibid.*) Harry's dead; Harry's been dead for years.

A

(*With increasing self-absorption.*) I know; so's everybody. I don't have any friends anymore; most of them are dead, and the ones aren't dead are dying, and the ones aren't dying have moved away or I don't see anymore.

B

(*Comforting.*) Well, what does it matter? You don't like any of them anymore anyway.

A

(*Uncomplicated agreement.*) That's true. But you're supposed to like them, to have them with you. Isn't it a
contract? You take people as friends and you spend
time at it, you put effort in, and it doesn't matter if
you don't like them anymore—who likes anybody anymore?—you've put in all that time, and what right do
they have to . . . to . . .

C

(*Incredulous.*) To die?!

A

What?!

C

What right do they have to die?

A

No! To not be what they were.

C

To change, you mean?

B

(*Gently.*) Let her alone.

A

No! No right! You count on them! And they change.
The Bradleys! The Phippses! They die; they go away.
And family dies; family goes away. Nobody should *do*
this! Look at Sis!

B

What about her?

A

My sister was a drunk.

(*Not friendly.*) She was smarter than me . . . no:
brighter, two years younger.

                                   C
(*Smiles.*) Or five, or seven.

                                   A
What?!

                                   C
Nothing.

                                   A
She always got better grades, had more beaux—when
we were growing up. Only then; she missed more boats
than you can shake a stick at.

                                   C
(*Examining her nails.*) I've never shook a stick at a boat.

                                   B
(*Dry.*) Well, maybe you should give it a try. Shaken; not
shook.

                                   A
We came to the city together, after she finished school,
and we had a tiny little apartment, and our mother and
our father came to see it, to be sure it was all right,
not dangerous, I suppose. It was furnished, but he
didn't like it, so he gave us some of theirs, some from
the garage. He made the most beautiful furniture: he
was an architect. We went out all the time—looking
for jobs, jobs that a young lady could accept—being
escorted out at night. We were the same size, so we
could wear each other's clothes; *that* saved money. We
had a little allowance, but a very little one, nothing to
spoil us. She was a little shorter, but not much. We kept
a list so the boys—the young men, the men—who took

us out—we went out with them together a lot—
wouldn't know we were wearing each other's. Is that
what I mean?

B

Yes; I think so; most probably.

C

Keep awake.

A

"No, no, I wore that at the Plaza; don't you remember?
You'd better wear the beads." We had a regular list.
We had big feet. (*A silence.*)

B

(*About the non sequitur.*) What?!

C

They had big *feet.*

A

We had big feet. I still do . . . I guess. (*To B.*) Do I still
have big feet?

B

Yes; yes, you do.

A

Well, I'd never know. I think we liked each other. We
used to confide a lot, and laugh, and . . . Mother made
us write twice a week—or call, later. We tried sending
letters together—one letter together—but she'd make
us send two—each of us one. They had to be newsy,
and long, and she'd send them back to us with things
like That's not true, or Don't abbreviate, or Your sister
said the same thing, if she didn't like them. Or spell-
ing. Sis couldn't spell. She drank.

C
(*Incredulous.*) Your mother?!

A
What?! No, of course not. My *sister*!

B
Of course.

C
Even then?

A
When?

C
When you . . . when you first came to the city.

A
No, of course not! Later. Well, we'd have champagne
when we went out—before the speakeasies. We would
drink champagne and nibble on candied orange rind.
He brings me some, sometimes, when he comes. Or
flowers—freesia, when they're in season. It's the least
he can do. And he *knows* it!

C
(*To* B; *and aside.*) Who? Who *is* this?

B
(*Absorbed with* A.) Shhhhhhh. Her son.

A
We'd go out, but we didn't take each other's boy-
friends. She was prim; I liked . . . wilder men, I suppose.

C

Tsk, tsk, tsk.

B

(*To* C; *amused.*) Why? Don't you?

A

We never liked the same boys . . . men. I don't think
she liked men very much. Well, I *know* she didn't—sex,
anyway. We had to make her get married, when she
was almost forty—*get* someone for her. I don't think
she wanted him; he was a wop.

C

(*Shakes her head.*) I don't believe it sometimes.

B

(*Sharp, as* A *tries to adjust herself in her chair.*) Why not?
Wop, nigger, kike? I told you: It doesn't *mean* anything.
It's the way she learned things.

C

From these strict but fair parents. (B *shrugs.*)

A

(*She has heard.*) I have Jewish friends, and I have Irish
friends, and I have South American friends—I *did.* Not
Puerto Rican, or like that, but Venezuelan, and Cuban.
Oh, we loved to go to Havana.

C

(*To* B, *more or less.*) Another world, eh?

B

Uh-huh.

A

I've never known any colored—well, *help*, yes. In Pine-
hurst they had colored help and we used to visit them

there. They knew their place; they were polite, and well behaved; none of those uppity niggers, the city ones.

C

(*Dismay.*) Oh, Jesus Christ!

A

He keeps telling me I can't say these things. I don't know what things he means. He said once he wouldn't come to see me anymore if I said those things. I don't know what things he means. What did he mean?

B

Don't worry yourself. Your sister married an *Italian*.

A

(*Confused.*) She did . . . what? Oh, that was later. I always had my eye out for the right man.

C

And she didn't?

A

No; she always thought everything would fall right into her lap. And it *did*; a *lot*. I had to work for *everything*; nothing came my way. I was tall and handsome; she was tall and pretty, tall but shorter, not as tall as I am . . . was. (*Weeps.*) I've shrunk! I'm not tall! I used to be so tall! Why have I shrunk?!

B

(*To* A; *patient.*) It happens with time: we get shorter. It happens every day, too: we're taller in the morning than we are at night.

A

(*Still weeping.*) How?!

B

The spine compresses as the day goes on.

A

(*Even weepier.*) I don't *have* one. I used to have a spine;
I don't have one anymore!

C

(*To* B*; sotto voce.*) What does she mean?

B

She means osteoporosis.

A

(*To* C*; ugly; weeping down to sniveling.*) It hasn't happened to you yet? You wait!

B

. . . the spine collapses; you can fracture it by walking,
turning around . . . whatever.

A

(*Weepy again.*) I used to be *tall*! I've shrunk!

C

I know.

(B *smiles.*)

A

(*Off again.*) *He* was *short.* A lot of my beaux were tall,
but he was short.

C

(*Sotto voce; to* B.) Who *is* this?

B

(*Sotto voce, too.*) Her husband, I think.

C

Oh; that's a long time ago.

A

Oh, I knew such tall boys, such dancers. Sis and I would dance all night with all the tall boys. Some of them were showboys—they were fairies—but some of them were regular. We would dance the night away; and sometimes I'd go off.

B

(*Smiling.*) Naughty girl!

A

I was the wild one. Sis would say to me, How can you *do* that?! and I'd laugh and I'd say, Oh, come on! I liked to have a good time, but I had my eye out. I always had my eye out. (*A shift of tone toward bitter.*) If I don't have my eye out, who will? I've always had to be on my toes, them sneaking around, stealing and . . . conniving. If I didn't keep my eye out we wouldn't have had *any*thing. His *sister*! That one she married? The first one! The dumpy little . . . dentist was he? What did *he* know about running an office? What did *he* know about handling money? Enough to steal! Enough to line his *own* pockets. And of course the old man kept his head turned the other way because the—what's his name, the dentist—was married to his precious daughter! Oh *that* one! Whining and finagling, wrapping him around her little finger! I had to stay one step ahead of *all* of them. I fixed 'em.

B

(*Proud of her.*) *Did* you?

A

(*Confused.*) What?!

B

Did you fix them?

A

(*Panicking.*) Who?! Who are you talking about?!

B

The ones you fixed.

A

How do *I* know? I don't know what you're talking about! Fix who?!

B

I don't *know.*

C

(*To help.*) The ones who were robbing you blind.

B

(*To* A.) Yes: those.

A

(*Grim.*) *Every*body's robbing me—right and left. Everybody steals. Everybody steals *some*thing.

B

(*Without comment.*) Including me? Do *I* steal?

A

(*Nervous laugh.*) I don't know. How would I know? He says I should have more money.

B

(*To* C.) Doesn't your office . . . ?

C

We deal with what comes *in.* There's more than one handles her money. There's plenty of chance, if anyone *wanted* to.

A

Sis used to envy me after I married. She never *did* well.
I always had my eye out.

C

You use all your income as far as *I* can see.

A

Well, why not? It's mine.

C

Well, just don't complain. If you wanted an increase in
principal, you'd have to . . .

A

I don't complain: I *never* complain. I have you, and I
have her (*points to* B), and I have the chauffeur, and I
have this place here, and I have to look pretty, and
sometimes I have the nurses—though they're black.
Why *is* that?—and I have all those things . . . I have
the cook, I have the . . .

C

I know; I know.

A

They all steal; every one of them.

B

(*After a pause, a sigh.*) Ah, well.

A

Sis didn't have her eye out; not like I did. I married
him. He was short; he had one eye; one was glass; a
golf ball hit him there; they took it out; he had a glass
one.

C

Which eye?

B

(*To* C; *chiding.*) Oh, *come* on!

C

(*Amused.*) No, I want to know. (*To* A.) Which eye?
Which eye was glass?

A

Which eye was . . . ? Well, I don't . . . (*becomes weepy*) I
can't remember! I don't know which eye was the glass
one! (*Full weep.*) I . . . can't . . . remember. I . . .
can't . . . remember!

B

(*Moves to* A, *to comfort.*) Now, now; now, now.

A

I can't remember! (*Sudden venom.*) Get your *hands* off
me! How *dare* you!

B

(*Retreating.*) Sorry; sorry.

A

(*To* B; *tearful again.*) Why can't I remember anything?

B

I think you remember everything; I think you just can't
bring it to mind all the time.

A

(*Quieting.*) Yes? Is that it?

B

Of course!

                                    A

I remember everything?

                                    B

Somewhere in there.

                                    A

(*Laughs.*) My gracious! (*To* C.) I remember everything!

                                    C

Gracious. That must be a burden.

                                    B

Be nice.

                                    C

Isn't salvation in forgetting? Lethe, and all?

                                    A

Who?

                                    B

No one.

                                    C

Lethe.

                                    A

I don't *know* her. Well, maybe I do, I just don't have it
right now. (*To* B.) Is that right?

                                    B

That's *right.*

                                    A

I *loved* my husband. (*Silly, remembering smile.*)

B

I bet you *did.*

A

He gave me pretty things; he gave me jewelry.

B

Them's pretty.

A

My God, he said, you're so big, so tall, you'll cost me
a fortune! I can't give you little things. And he *couldn't.*
I liked pearls and diamonds best.

C

No kidding!

B

(*Amused.*) Oh, hush!

A

I had my pearls, and I had some bracelets, and he
wanted me to have another—he'd found one without
telling me. We wore wide bracelets back then—diamond ones—wide, *this* wide. (*She demonstrates: two
inches, or so.*) Flat and wide, the stones in designs,
very . . . what? Very what?

B

Ornate.

A

Yes, ornate . . . and wide. We had been out—I'll never
forget it, I'll never forget this—we'd been to a party,
and we'd had champagne, and we were . . . what?
Tipsy? A little I suppose. And we came home and we

were on the way to bed. We had our big bedroom, and
it had its separate dressing rooms, and—you know—
its separate bathrooms—and we were undressing; we
were getting ready for bed. I was at my table, and I'd
taken off my clothes—my shoes, my dress, and my
underthings—and I was sitting there at my dressing
table (*She really enjoys telling this: laughs, giggles, etc.*), and
I was . . . well, I was naked; I didn't have a stitch, except
I had on all my jewelry. I hadn't taken off my jewelry.

B

How wonderful!

A

Yes! And there I was, all naked with my pearls—my
necklace—and my bracelets, my diamond bracelets . . .
two, no: three! Three! And in he walked, naked as a
jaybird—he was funny when he wanted to be—we were
naked a lot, early on, pretty early on. All that stopped.
(*Pause.*) Where am I?

B

In your story?

A

What?

B

In your story. Where are you in your story?

A

Yes; of course.

C

You're naked at your dresser, and *he* walks in, and *he's*
naked, too.

A

. . . as a jaybird; yes! Oh, I shouldn't *tell* this!

B

Yes! Yes, you should!

C

Yes!

A

Yes? Oh . . . well, there I was, and I had my big powder
puff, and I was powdering myself, and I was paying
attention to *that*. I knew he was there, but I wasn't paying attention. I *have* something for you, he said, I *have*
something for you. And I was sitting there, and I raised
my eyes and looked in the mirror and . . . no! I can't
tell this!

B & C

(*Silly schoolgirls.*) Yes, yes; tell, tell. Tell us! Yes! Tell us!
(*This ad lib.*)

A

And I looked and there he was, and his . . . his pee-
pee was all hard, and . . . and hanging on it was a new
bracelet.

C

(*Awe.*) Oh, my God!

(B *smiles.*)

A

And it was on his pee-pee, and he came close and it
was the most beautiful bracelet I'd ever seen; it was
diamonds, and it was wide, so wide and . . . I thought
you might like this, he said. Oh, my goodness, it's so
beautiful, I said. Do you want it? he said. Yes, yes! I

said, Oh, goodness, yes! (*Mood shifts a little toward dark-
ness.*) And he came closer, and his pee-pee touched my
shoulder—he was short, and I was tall, or something.
Do you want it? he said, and he poked me with it, with
his pee-pee, and I turned, and he had a little pee-pee.
Oh, I shouldn't say that; that's terrible to say, but I
know. He had a little . . . *you* know . . . and there was
the bracelet on it, and he moved closer, to my face,
and Do you want it? I thought you might like it. And
I said, No! I can't *do* that! You *know* I can't *do* that! and
I couldn't; I could *never* do that, and I said, No! I can't
do that! And he stood there for . . . well, I don't
know . . . and his pee-pee got . . . well, it started to go
soft, and the bracelet slid off, and it fell into my lap. I
was naked; deep into my lap. Keep it, he said, and he
turned and he walked out of my dressing room.

(*Long silence; finally she weeps, slowly, conclusively.*)

B
(*Eventually.*) It's all right; it's all right.

(*Goes and comforts* A.)

C
(*Kindly*) The wild one.

B
(*Still comforting.*) It's all right; it's all right.

A
(*Little child.*) Take me to bed; take me to bed.

B
Sure. (*To* C.) Help me.

(*They ease her up from her chair and to the bed during the
following.*)

A

(*Screams.*) My arm! My arm!

C

(*Terrified.*) I'm sorry!

A

Bed! I wanna go to bed!

B

All right now; we're almost there. (*At bed.*) OK. Here
we are.

A

(*Full baby.*) I wanna go to bed! (*It hurts!*) Oh! Oh! Oh!

B

All right, now. (A *is now on the bed, under covers, sitting
up part way.*) There. Comfy?

C

(*To* B.) I'm sorry; I didn't mean to . . .

B

(*To* C.) It's all right. (*To* A.) Comfy?

A

(*Tiny voice.*) Yes. Thank you.

B

(*As she moves downstage.*) You're welcome.

C

I'm not good at . . . all that.

B

You'll get there.

C

I can't pro*ject*.

B

(*Comforting.*) Well, think of it this way: if you live long
enough you won't have to; you'll be there.

C

Thanks.

B

And since it's the far past we're supposed to recall
best—if we *get* to the future—you'll re*mem*ber not being able to project.

C

As I said: thanks.

B

(*Pause; sighs.*) A-ha.

C

(*Pause.*) What happens now?

B

(*Eyes closed.*) You tell *me*.

C

You're the one works here.

B

(*Smiles; eyes still closed.*) As I said: *you* tell *me*. (*Silence.*)

A

(*Propped up; eyes opening and closing from time to time, eyes
wandering; very stream of consciousness.*) The things we're
able to do and the things we're *not*. What we remember
doing and what we're not sure. What do I re*mem*ber?

I remember being *tall*. I remember first it making me
unhappy, being taller in my class, taller than the boys.
I remember, and it comes and goes. I think they're all
robbing me. I *know* they are, but I can't prove it. I think
I know, and then I can't remember what I know. (*Cries
a little.*) He never comes to see me.

B

(*Mildly.*) *Yes*, he does.

A

When he has to; now and then.

B

More than most; he's a good son.

A

(*Tough.*) Well, I don't know about that. (*Softer.*) He
brings me things; he brings me flowers—orchids, freesia, those big violets . . . ?

B

African.

A

Yes. He brings me those, and he brings me choc-
olates—orange rind in chocolate, that dark chocolate
I like; he does *that*. But he doesn't love me.

B

Oh, now.

A

He doesn't! He loves his . . . he loves his boys, those
boys he has. You don't know! He doesn't love me and
I don't know if I love him. I can't *remember*!

B

He loves you.

A

(*Near tears.*) I can't remember; I can't remember what
I can't remember. (*Suddenly alert and self-mocking.*) Isn't
that something!

B

(*Nicely.*) It certainly *is.*

A

(*Rambling again.*) There's so much: holding on; fight-
ing for everything; *he* wouldn't do it; *I* had to do *every*thing; tell him how handsome he was, clean up his
blood. Everything came on *me*: Sis being that way, hid-
ing her bottles in her night things where she thought
I wouldn't find them when she came to stay with me
for a little; falling . . . falling down the way she did.
Mother coming to stay, to live with us; he *said* she
could; where else could she go? Did we like each other
even? At the end? Not at the end, not when she hated
me. I'm helpless, she . . . she screamed; I hate you!
She stank; her room stank; she stank; I hate you, she
screamed at me. I think they all hated me, because I
was strong, because I *had* to be. Sis hated me; Ma hated
me; all those others, *they* hated me; *he* left home; he
ran away. Because I was strong. I was tall and I was
strong. *Somebody* had to be. If I wasn't, then . . . (*Silence;*
A *still, eyes open. Has she shuddered a little before her
silence?*)

(*After a bit* B *and* C *look at one another.* B *rises, goes to the
bed, leans over, gazes at* A, *feels her pulse.*)

C

(*Looks over after a little.*) Is she . . . oh, my God, is she
dead?

B

(*After a little.*) No. She's alive. I think she's had a stroke.

C

Oh, my God!

B

You better call her son. I'll call the doctor.

(C *rises, exits right, looking at* A *as she exits;* B *strokes* A*'s head, exits left.*)

(A *alone; still; silence.*)

END OF ACT ONE

ACT TWO

"A" is propped up in bed. (Actually a life mask of the actress playing A—wearing exact, same costume as on A in Act One. We must believe it to be A—a breathing mask over the nose and mouth helps this.)

When A appears she is dressed in a lovely, lavender dress.

(*Some silence.* B *and* C *enter, opposite from their exits at the end of Act One. They—and* A, *when she enters—are dressed differently from the way they were at the end of Act One, except that the dummy of* A *is dressed as* A *was at the end of Act One.* C *seats herself.* B *goes to the bed, looks at* "A.")

B

(*General.*) No change.

C

(*Wistful.*) No?

B

That's the way it goes.

C

(*Shudders.*) Yes?

B

(*Grim.*) Something to look forward to. (*No response from* C.) No?

C

(*Hard.*) I don't want to *talk* about it; I don't want to *think* about it. Let me alone.

B

(*Sharp.*) It's worth thinking about—even at *your* age.

C

Let me *alone!*

B

(*Wandering about; touching things.*) It's got to be *some* way . . . stroke, cancer or, as the lady said, heading into a

mountain with a jet. No? (*No response.*) *Or* . . . walking
off a curb into a sixty-mile-an-hour wall . . .

C

Stop it!

B

Or . . . even worse; *think* about this . . . home alone in
the evening, servants off, him out, at the club, sitting
home alone, the window jimmied, *they* get in, little cat
feet and all, *find* you, sitting there in the upstairs sitting
room . . .

C

I said: *stop* it!

B

(*Smiles.*) . . . find me sitting there in the upstairs sitting
room, going over invitations, or whatever . . . bills;
come up behind me, slit my throat, me thinking, Oh,
my God, my throat's being slit, *if* that, if there's *time*
for that.

C

(*Animal growl of protest.*) Arghhhhhhhhhh!

B

(*Tranquil.*) I'm almost done. Or I hear them . . . you
hear them turn around, see them—how many? Two?
Three?—fall apart, start screaming, so they have to slit
your throat, my throat, though they may not have
planned it that way. All that blood on the Chinese rug.
My, my.

C

(*Pause; curious.*) Chinese rug?

B

(*Very natural.*) Yes, beige, with rose embroidery all around the edges. We get it at auction.

C

I wouldn't know.

B

(*Momentary surprise.*) No; of course not; you *wouldn't.* You will, though—the rug, I mean. Clearly nobody slits your throat, or mine, for that matter. (*Considers it.*) Might be better.

C

(*Rue and helplessness.*) You have things to tell me, I suppose.

B

Oh, I certainly do. But, then again, I don't know everything either, *do* I. (*Gestures towards* A.)

C

(*She looks, too.*) I'll do a will; I'll do some paper that won't let me go on if I get like that.

B

There *aren't* any . . . *weren't* any then, I tried. You can't get your way in this world.

(A *enters during this next speech, from stage left.*)

C

There *must* be one. You have your way in everything and then you can't at the last? There *must* be!

A

There *must* be what?

(*She is thoroughly rational during this act;* B *and* C *are not surprised to see her.*)

C

A living will.

A

(*Observing* "A.") I was going to, but then I forgot, or it slipped my mind, or something. He kept saying, Make one! He has one for himself, he says. I meant to; nothing much to do about it now. Any change?

B

No, we're . . . just as we were; no change.

A

I wonder how long *this'll* go on. I hope it's quick. What's-her-name took six years; not a move, not a blink, hooked up, breathed for, pissed for.

B

Do I know her?

A

No; after your time, so to speak.

B

A-*ha.*

A

A lot of money—a *lot.* The kids—hah! Fifty the youngest—the "kids" disagreed. They wanted to see the will first, the lawyer wouldn't *show* it to 'em, they came down on both sides—*kill* her off! keep her going! Not pretty.

C

(*Really beside herself.*) Stop it! Stop it!

A

(*To a naughty child.*) Grow . . . up.

B

(*Smiles.*) She will; she does.

A

Well; yes; of course. And so do *you*.

C

(*Rage.*) I will not become . . . *that*! (*Points to* "A.")

A

(*Come off it.*) Oh, ́really.

B

(*Oh, really!*) Come *off* it.

C

I *won't*.

B

(*Smiles.*) What do you plan to *do* about it?

A

(*Amused.*) Yes; *that's* interesting.

C

(*To* A; *pointing to* B.) Nor will I become *this*.

B

(*A hoot.*) Hah!

C

(*To the audience, unless otherwise indicated; she comes down front.* A *and* B *relax, comment from time to time, react with each other, etc.*) I *won't*. I *know* I won't—*that's* what I mean. That . . . (*points to* "A") . . . *thing* there? I'll never

be like that. (B *hoots;* A *shakes her head, chuckles.*) *Nobody*
could. I'm twenty-six; I'm a *good* girl; my mother was
strict but fair—she still *is;* she *loves* me; she loves me
and Sis, and she wants the very best for us. We have a
nice little apartment, Sis and I, and at night we go out
with our beaux, and I *do* have my eye out for . . . for
what—the man of my dreams? And so does Sis, I *guess.*
I don't think I've been in love, but I've been loved—
by a couple of them, but they weren't the right ones.

B
(*Rue; to herself.*) They never *are.*

A
(*Purring.*) Hmmmm.

C
Mother taught us what the right one would be. We
have fun with the others—dancing, staying out late,
seeing the sun up sometimes. Things get a little . . .
involved now and again, and that's fun too, though Sis
doesn't think so as much as I do. They get involved,
but they never get very . . . *serious.* I have my eye out,
and we do have our *jobs.* We're mannequins: the fan-
ciest shop in town!

B
I don't want that *known!*

A
(*To* B; *pleasantly chiding.*) Oh, stop; it was fun.

C
We go into work and we put on these lovely frocks, and
we walk elegantly around the store (*imitates*), among
the ladies shopping, sometimes with their men, sometimes not, and we stop, and they touch our dresses—
the silk, the fabric—and they ask us questions, and

then we pass on to another group, to another section.
We twirl, we . . . sashay. (*Does so;* B *imitates;* A, *too, but*
sitting.)

(*To* A *and* B.) We *do*!

                          B
Oh, I *know.*

                          A
Yes, we *know*; do *we know.*

                          C
(*To the audience again.*) Don't look at them; don't . . .
listen to them. (A *and* B laugh a little.) We wear our
beautiful evening gowns, and we parade about, and we
know there are people looking at us, studying us, and
we smile, and we . . . well, I suppose we flirt a little
with the men who are doing it—the husbands, or
whatever.

                          B
(*To* A; *mock astonishment.*) Flirt?! You?!

                          A
Me?! Flirt?!

                          B
(*Sashays; twirls.*) Wheeeee!

                          A
(*Claps with one hand; her knee, probably.*) Brava! Brava!

                          B
(*Twirls.*) Wheeeee!

                          C
Stop it! *Stay* out of my life!

B

Oh! My dear!

A

(*To* C.) I remember it differently, little one. I remember more . . . design. I remember a little calculation.

B

Oh, yes; a little calculation; a little design.

C

(*To audience.*) Don't listen to them. Design? What are they talking about?

B

(*Cheerful.*) Never mind.

C

(*To audience.*) They don't *know* me!

B

(*Looking at* A; *mocking.*) Noooooooooooo!

C

Remember me!

A

(*Ibid.*) Noooooooooooo! (C *claps her hands over her ears, shuts her eyes.*) Oh, all right, dear; go on. (C *can't hear; louder.*) I said, go *on!*

B

(*Loud.*) She says go *on!* Honestly.

C

I am a . . . good . . . girl.

B

(*To* A.) Well, yes; I suppose so.

A

And not dumb.

C

I'm a good girl. I know how to attract *men*. I'm *tall*;
I'm striking; *I* know how to do it. Sis slouches and
caves her front in; I stand tall, breasts out, chin up,
hands . . . just so. I walk between the aisles and they
know there's somebody coming, that there's somebody
there. But, I'm a *good girl.* I'm not a virgin, but I'm a
good girl. The boy who took me was a good boy.

(C *does not necessarily hear—or, at least, notice—the asides
to come.*)

B

Oh, yes he *was*.

A

Yes? Was he?

B

You remember.

A

(*Laughs.*) Well, it *was* a *while* ago.

B

But you *do* remember.

A

Oh yes, I remember him. He was . . .

C

. . . sweet and handsome; no, not handsome: beautiful.
He was beautiful!

A

(*To* B.) He was; yes.

B

(*To* A *and herself.*) Yes.

C

He has coal black hair and violet eyes and such a smile!

A

Ah!

B

Yes!

C

His body was . . . well, it was thin, but *hard*; all sinew
and muscle; he fenced, he told me, and he was the one
with the megaphone on the crew. When I held him
when we danced, there was only sinew and muscle. We
dated a lot; I liked him; I didn't tell Mother, but I liked
him a lot. I like him, Sis, I said; I really like him. Have
you told mother? No, and don't *you*; I like him a lot,
but I don't *know*. Has he? . . . *you* know. No, I said, no,
he hasn't. But then he did. We were dancing—slowly
—late, the end of the evening, and we danced so close,
all . . . pressed, and . . . we were pressed, and I could
feel that he was hard, *that* muscle and sinew, pressed
against me while we danced. We were the same height
and he looked into my eyes as we danced, slowly, and
I felt the pressure up against me, and he tensed it and
I felt it move against me.

B

(*Dreamy.*) Whatever is *that*? I said.

A

Hmmmmmmmm.

C

Whatever is *that*? I said. I *knew*, but Whatever is that, I said, and he smiled, and his eyes shone, and, It's me in love with you, he said. You have an interesting way of showing it, I said. Appropriate, he said, and I felt the muscle move again, and . . . well, I knew it was time; I knew I was ready, and I knew I wanted him—whatever that *meant*—that I wanted *him*, that I wanted *it.*

B

(*Looking back; agreeing.*) Yes; oh, yes.

A

Hmmmmmmmmmmm.

C

Remember, don't give it away, Mother said; don't give it away like it was nothing.

B

(*Remembering.*) They won't respect you for it and you'll get known as a loose girl. *Then* who will you marry?

A

(*To* B.) Is that what she said? I can't remember.

B

(*Laughs.*) *Yes* you can.

C

They won't respect you for it and you'll get known as a loose girl. *Then* who will you marry? But he was

pressed against me, exactly against where he wanted to
be—we were the same height—and he was *so* beautiful,
and his eyes shone, and he smiled at me and he moved
his hips as we danced, so slowly, as we danced, and he
breathed on my neck and he said, You don't want me
to embarrass myself right here on the dance floor, do
you?

B

(*Remembering.*) No, no; of course not.

C

I said, No, no; of course not. Let's go to my place, he
said, and I heard myself saying (*incredulous*), I'm not
that kind of girl? I mean, as soon as I said it I blushed:
it was so . . . stupid, so . . . expected. Yes, you are, he
said; *you're* that kind of girl.

B

And I was, and my God it was wonderful.

A

It hurt! (*Afterthought: to* B.) Didn't it?

B

(*Admonishing.*) Oh . . . well, a little.

C

You're that kind of girl, and I guess I was. We did it a
lot. (*Shy.*) I know it's trite to say your first time is your
best, but he was wonderful, and I know I'm only twenty-
six now and there've been a few others, and I imagine
I'll marry, and I'll be very happy.

B

(*Grudging.*) Well . . .

A

We'll talk about happy sometime.

C

I *know* I'll be very happy, but will I ever *not* think about
him? He was long and thick and knew what I wanted,
what I needed, and while I couldn't do . . . you know:
the thing he wanted . . . I just *couldn't*. I *can't*.

B

(*Stretches.*) Nope; never could.

A

(*Sort of dreamy.*) I wonder why.

C

(*Very agitated; upset.*) I tried! I wanted to do what . . .
but I choked, and I . . . (*whispered*) I threw up. I
just . . . couldn't.

A

(*To* c.) Don't worry about it; don't worry about what
can't be helped.

B

And . . . there's more than one way to skin a cat.

A

(*Puzzles that.*) Why?

B

Hm?

A

Why is there more than one way to skin a *cat*?

B

(*Puzzles that.*) Why not?

A

Who needs it?! Isn't one way *enough?*

C

(*To the audience; still; simply.*) I just want you to know that I'm a good girl, that I was a good girl.

B

(*To* C.) You meet him in two years.

C

(*Self-absorbed.*) What? Who?

B

(*Pleasant.*) Your husband. We're what—twenty-six? We'll meet him in two years.

C

(*Making light of it.*) The man of my dreams?

B

Well, a man you'll *dream* about.

A

For a long, long time.

C

Like the boy I was . . . ?

A

Well, yes, he was wonderful, but then there's life.

B

(*To* A.) *How* long?

A

Hm?

B

How *long*?

A

Long enough. (*To* B.) You're . . . what?

B

Fifty-two.

A

(*Calculating.*) I marry when I'm twenty-eight; you're sixty-six when he dies. (*To* C; *smiles.*) We have him a good long time.

B

(*Musing.*) Another fourteen years.

A

Yes, but the last *six* aren't much fun.

C

That's almost forty years with one man.

B

(*To* C; *chuckles.*) Well, more or less: more or less one man. (*To* A.) No? Not much fun?

A

Not much.

C

How *is* he? Have I *met* him?

B

The one-eyed man? The little one; the little one-eyed man?

A

(*Chuckles.*) Oh, now.

C

(*Confused.*) What?

B

The one we meet at the party—Sis and me. Sis is with
him, but I see him looking over at me.

A

(*Recalled with pleasure.*) Yes!

B

Sis doesn't much care, I don't think.

C

More or less? What is this more or less?

A

Hm?

B

(*Mildly annoyed.*) I beg your pardon?

C

I said almost forty years with one man; you said, more
or less; more or less one man.

B

Oh? Ah! Well, what are you expecting? Monogamy or
something?

C

Yes! If I care: yes!

B

(*To* A.) Remember monogamy?

A

(*Pretends to puzzle it.*) No. (*New tone; to* B.) *You* can talk
about monogamy, if you like—pro and con, if you like.
Leave me out of *that* one.

B

(*General, then to* A.) Infidelity is a matter of spirit—isn't
that what they say? Aside from bad taste, disease, confusion as to where you live, having to lie all the
time—*and* remember the lies! God, remember the lies?

A

Hmmmm. Well, there wasn't much, not *too* much.

B

Except for the groom, eh?

A

Oh, my! The groom.

C

Why do I marry him?

B

Who—the groom? (A *and* B *laugh.*)

C

The one-eyed man! I marry the one-eyed man!

B

Yes, you do.

C

Why?!

B

(*To* C.) Why do I *marry* him? Why did I *marry* him?
(*To* A.)

A

(*To* B.) Why did I?

B

Hmmmmmmmmm.

C

.*Tell* me!

B

Because he makes me *laugh*. Because he's little and he's funny looking—and a little like a penguin.

A

(*Has she thought this before?*) Yes! Quite a bit like one.

B

(*Generous.*) Well . . . especially in his bib and tucker.

C

(*Some panic.*) Why would I marry him if I'm going to cheat on *him*?!

A

(*Smiles.*) Why would you marry him if he's going to cheat on *you*?

C

I don't *know*!

B

Calm down; adjust; settle in. Men cheat; men cheat a *lot*. We cheat *less*, and we cheat because we're lonely; men cheat because they're men.

A

No. We cheat because we're bored, sometimes. We cheat to get back; we cheat because we don't know any

better; we cheat because we're whores. *We* cheat for *lots*
of reasons. Men cheat for only one—as you say, because they're men.

C

Tell me about him!

A

Don't you want to be surprised?

C

No!

B

You've seen him, or . . . he's seen *you*. I don't think
you've met him. He's something of what they call a
playboy—at least in *my* time, not yours. He's rich—or
his father is—and he's divorcing his second wife; she's
just plain bad; the first one drank; still does.

A

That one dies eventually—eighty, or something: pick-
led; preserved.

C

(*Timid again.*) What's he like?

B

(*Expansive.*) Well . . . he's short, and he has one eye,
and he's a great dancer—'cept he keeps running into
things, the eye, you know—and he sings like a dream!
A lovely tenor—and he's funny! God, he's funny!

A

(*Wistful.*) Yes; yes, he was.

B

(*Pleased.*) And he likes tall women!

A

(*Wistful.*) Yes; yes, he did.

C

(*Uncertain.*) I *have seen* him?

B

He tells me—I think I remember—he tells me he saw
me with Sis before he dated her, that I was taller, that
he had—you'll forgive the joke—his eye on me. (*To*
A.) Didn't he tell you that—that he had his eye on us?

A

I can't remember. He was going with that comedienne
did the splits, the eight-foot one.

B

Well, you put a stop to that soon enough.

A

Once you got your claws into him you mean?

C

(*Puzzling.*) Why did I *like* him? Is funny enough? Is having a voice, is dancing enough?

B

Don't forget one eye.

A

Oh, he was *nice*; we liked him a lot.

C

Liked? Liked him a lot.

B

(*Looking right at* C.) Oh, stop it! You're twenty-six years
old, which is not a tot; there *is* the future to look out
for . . .

A

. . . and he *is* rich, or is going to be: rich family.

C

I don't *believe* this.

A

(*Sharp.*) Our father *dies*.

B

(*About her father.*) I *loved him.*

C

No! He doesn't!

B

*Every*body does.

A

(*To herself.*) Except me, maybe.

B

(*To* C.) Except *us.*

C

I *love* him!

B

Well, that should be enough to keep the old heart going: Jesus, she loves me; how can I go and die on her?

C

Is it . . . quick?

A

(*Pensive.*) I don't remember.

B

Not bad: heart *failure*, fluid in the lungs, some bad breathing; oh, God, the terror in the eyes! (C *begins to weep;* B *notices.*) We did that, yes. We cried when Dad died. I cried; Sis cried; Mom went out on the porch and did it there.

A

(*Loss.*) I don't remember.

C

What happens to Ma?

B

She holds out; she stays on alone for almost twenty years, and then she moves in with us. (*To* A.) How does it *go*?

A

(*Toneless.*) What? She becomes an enemy. She dies when she's eighty-four—seventeen years of it, of staying up in her room in the big house with us. The colitis, the cigarettes, the six or seven Pekingese she goes through. I stopped liking her.

C

I *couldn't*!

A

(*Shrugs.*) She becomes an enemy.

B

(*Interested, but not too much.*) How?

A

(*Sighs.*) She comes to resent me; she starts to resent getting old, getting . . . helpless—the eyes, the spine, the mind. She starts to resent that I have—*we* have—so much, and that I'm being generous—*we're* being generous. She snaps at everything; she sides with Sis; she criticizes me.

B

(*Some awe.*) She wasn't *like* that.

C

No! She *couldn't* be.

A

I don't care. Forget I told you. She never moved in; she's still alive up there in the country, in the same house; she's a hundred and thirty-seven now, does her own baking, jogs three times a week . . .

B

All right; *all* right.

A

(*To* B.) There's more. You want to hear it? (B *shakes her head to* C.) Of course *you* don't. (C *shakes her head.*) No, of course not. Anyhow, you marry him.

C

(*Getting it straight.*) I do.

A

Yes; he's fun, and he's nice.

B

He sings . . .

A

He dances . . .

B

. . . and he's rich, or going to be . . .

A

. . . and he loves tall women.

B

And you suddenly realize you love short men.

A

Penguins. (A *and* B *both giggle.*)

B

(*Still to* C.) *And* it goes all right. His mother doesn't *like* me—doesn't *like* you—at all, but the old *man* does.

A

He certainly does! You're tall; I bet you're hot stuff.

B

(*To* C.) You win him over. (*To* A.) You know, I think the old buzzard had letch for us?

A

Yes; *I* think so.

B

And, boy did he want a *grand*son.

A

Oh, that made him happy.

C

(*Wonder.*) I have children?

B

(*None too pleasant.*) We have one; we have a boy.

A

(*Same.*) Yes, we do. I have a son.

(*He appears in the stage right archway, stands stock still, stares at "*A*" on the bed.*)

B

(*Seeing him; sneering.*) Well, fancy seeing you again. (*Sudden, and enraged, into his face.*) Get out of my house! (*He doesn't react.*)

C

(*Rising.*) Stop it! (*Moves toward him.*) Is . . . is that him?

B

I said, get out of my house!

A

(*To* B.) Do be quiet. (*To* C.) Let him alone; he's come to see me. (*He goes to "*A*", sits on the bed stage right of her, either on the bed or on a chair, takes her right arm; shoulders shake, puts his forehead to her arm, or it to his forehead, becomes still. Does not react to anything about him until indicated.*) That's it; do your duty.

C

He's . . . my goodness. How nice; how handsome, how very . . .

B

You wouldn't say that if you knew!

A

Shhhhhhhh.

B

(*To* A.) She wouldn't! (*To him.*) Filthy little . . .

A

Shhhhh. Shhhhh. I don't want to think about *that*. He came back; he never loved me, he never loved us, but he came back. Let him alone.

C

He's so young.

A

Yes . . . well. This is how he looked when he went away, took his life and one bag and went off. (*To* B.) No?

B

(*To his back; less venom, but mixed with hurt.*) You wore that coat the day you left. I thought I told you to get your hair cut!

A

Yes; yes, he did; he wore that coat. I'm leaving, he said, and he took one bag. (*Pause.*) *And* his life.

C

(*Bewildered.*) He went away from me? Why?

B

(*Bitter.*) Maybe you changed; they say you changed; I haven't noticed. (*To* A.) He comes back? He comes back to me—to me? I let him?

A

Sure. We have a heart attack; they tell him; he comes back. Twenty plus years? That's a long enough sulk— on both sides. He didn't come back when his father died.

B

(*Scathing.*) Of course not!

A

But he came to me. They call me up and they tell me he's coming to see me; they say he's going to call. He calls. I hear his voice and it all floods back, but I'm formal. Well, hello there, I say. Hello there to you, he says. Nothing about this shouldn't have happened. Nothing about I've missed you, not even that little lie. Sis is visiting; she's lying drunk and passed out upstairs and not even that little lie. I thought I'd come over. Yes, you do that. He comes; we look at each other and we both hold in whatever we've been holding in since that day he went away. You're looking well, he says; and, You, too, I say. And there are no apologies, no recriminations, no tears, no hugs; dry lips on my dry cheeks; yes that. And we never discuss it? Never go into why? Never go beyond where we are? We're strangers; we're curious about each other; we leave it at that.

B

I'll *never* forgive him.

A

(*Wistful, sad.*) No; I never do. But we play the game. We dine; he takes me places—mother, son going to formal places. We never . . . reminisce. Eventually he lets me talk about when he was a little boy, but he never has an opinion on that; he doesn't seem to have an opinion on much of anything that has to do with us, with me.

B

(*Clenched teeth.*) Never!

A

(*To* B.) Or with *you.* (*To* C; *and sad smile.*) Or *you.*

C

Did we . . . did we drive him away? Did I change so?

B

(*Rage.*) He left!! He packed up his attitudes and he
left!! And I never want to see him again. (*To him.*) Go
away!! (*Angry, humiliated, tears.*)

A

(*Very calm; sad smile.*) Well, yes you *do*, you see. You *do*
want to see him again. *Wait* twenty years. Be alone except for her upstairs passed out on the floor, and the
piano top with the photos in the silver frames, and the
butler, and . . . be all alone; you *do* want to see him
again, but the terms are too hard. We never forgive
him. We let him come, but we never forgive him. (*To
him.*) I bet you don't know *that* . . . *do* you!

C

(*To* A.) How did we change? (*To him.*) How did I
change? (*He strokes "*A*'s" face, shudders a little.*)

B

Don't bother yourself. He *never* belonged.

C

(*Enraged.*) I don't believe it!

B

(*Furious.*) Let it *alone*!

C

No! How did I *change*?! What *happened* to me?!

A

(*Sighs.*) Oh, God.

C

(*Determined.*) How did I *change*?!

B

(*Sarcasm; to the audience.*) She wants to know how she *changed*. She wants to know how she turned into *me*. Next she'll want to know how I turned into *her*. (*Indicates* A.) No; I'll want to know *that*, *maybe* I'll want to know that.

A

Hahh!

B

Maybe. (*To* C.) You want to know how I changed?

C

(*Very alone.*) I don't know. *Do* I?

B

Twenty-six to fifty-two? Double it? Double your pleasure, double your fun? Try *this*. Try *this* on for size. They *lie* to you. You're growing up and they go out of their way to hedge, to qualify, to . . . to evade; to avoid—to *lie*. Never tell it how it is—how it's *going* to be—when a half-truth can be got in there. Never give the alternatives to the "pleasing prospects," the "what you have to look forward to." God, if they did the streets'd be littered with adolescent corpses! Myabe it's better they don't.

A

(*Mild ridicule.*) They? *They?*

B

Parents, teachers, all the others. You *lie* to us. You don't tell us things change—that Prince Charming has the morals of a sewer rat, that you're supposed to *live* with

that . . . *and* like it, or give the ap*pear*ance of liking it.
Chasing the chambermaid into closets, the kitchen
maid into the root cellar, and God knows *what* goes on
at the stag at the club! They probably nail the whores
to the billiard tables for easy access. Nobody *tells* you
any of this.

A

(*Lay it on.*) Poor, poor you.

C

The root cellar?

B

(*To* A *and* C.) Hush. No wonder one day we come back
from riding, the horse all slathered, snorting, and he
takes the reins, the groom does, and he helps us dis-
mount, the groom does, his hand touching the back
of our thigh, and we notice, and he notices we notice,
and we remember that we've noticed him before, most
especially bare chested that day heaving the straw,
those arms, that butt. And no wonder we smile in that
way he understands so quickly, and no wonder he leads
us into a further stall—into the fucking *hay*, for God's
sake!—and down we go, and it's revenge and self-pity
we're doing it for until we notice it turning into pleasure for its own sake, for *our* own sake, and we're drip-
ping wet and he rides us like we've seen in the pornos
and we actually scream, and then we lie there in the
straw—which probably has shit on it—cooling down,
and he tells us he's wanted us a lot, that he likes big
women, but he didn't dare, and will he get fired now?
And I say, No, no, of course you won't and for a month
more of it I don't, but then I do; I do have him fired,
because it's dangerous not to, because it's a good deal
I've got with the penguin, a long-term deal in spite of
the crap he pulls, and you'd better keep your nose
clean—or polished, anyway—for the *real* battles—for

the penguin's *other* lady folk, the *real* ones—the mother
who "just doesn't like you" for no good reason except
her daughter hates you, fears you and hates you—*en-
vies* and therefore hates you—dumpy, stupid, whining
little bitch! Just *doesn't* like you—maybe in part because
she senses the old man's got the letch for you and
besides, no girl's good enough for the penguin, not *her*
penguin; the first two sure weren't and this one's not
going to be either. Try to keep on the good side of the
whole wretched family, stand up for your husband
when he won't do it for himself, watch out for all the
intrigue; start *really* worrying about your sister who's
really stopped worrying about herself—about *anything;*
watch your own mother begin to change even more
than you're aware *you* are, and then try to raise that?!
(*Points to him.*) That?!—gets himself thrown out of
every school he can find, even one or two we haven't
sent him to, sense he hates you, catch him doing it
with your niece-in-law *and* your nephew-in-law the same
week?! Start reading the letters he's getting from—how
do they call it—older friends?—telling him how to out-
wit *you,* how to survive living with his awful family; tell
him you'll brain him with the fucking crystal ashtray if
he doesn't stop getting letters, doesn't stop saying anything, doesn't stop . . . just . . . doesn't . . . stop? And
he sneers, and he says very quietly that he can have me
put in jail for opening his mail. Not while you're a
minor, I tell him; you just wait, I tell him, you just wait;
I'll have you thrown out of this house so quick it'll
make your head spin. *You're* going to fire me, he says,
quietly, smiling; you going to *fire* me too? Just like you
fired *him?* He's good in bed, *isn't* he! Of course, *you*
wouldn't know about *bed,* he says. He gets up, stops by
me, touches my hair. I thought I saw some straw, he
says; sorry. And he walks out of the solarium, out of
the house, out of our lives. He doesn't say good-bye to
either of us. He says good-bye to Mother, upstairs; he
says good-bye to the Pekingese, too, I imagine. He

packs one bag, and he leaves. (*To him; rage.*) Get out
of my house!! (*Pause; to* C.) Does that tell you a little
something about change? Does that tell you what you
want to know?

C
(*Pause; softly.*) Yes. Thank you.

(*Silence.*)

A
(*Curious.*) You want some more?

C
No, thank you.

B
I shouldn't *think* so.

A
Yes, you *do*; you *want* more.

C
(*Trying to stay polite.*) I said, no, thank you.

A
That doesn't cut any ice around here. (*Points to* B.) How
you got to *her* is one thing; how you got to me is another. How do you put it . . . that *thing* there? (*Points
to* "A.")

C
I'm sorry.

A
Well . . . maybe.

B

Yeah, I've got a few doubts about *that* route myself.

A

You!

B

Yeah; well. I'm not so bad. There's been shit, but there've been *good* times, too. Some of the best.

A

(*Oddly bright.*) Of course; there are always good times: like when we broke our back. (*To* C.) You break your back.

B

(*Laughs a little.*) Yeah; you sure *do*.

C

(*Scared of this.*) I do?

B

Snap!

A

(*Smiles.*) Well, not exactly. Snap! Really!

B

I should *know*; it was *only* ten years ago, and . . .

A

Riding, yes; jumping. We never liked jumping—hunters. Saddle horses, yes, hunters, no. Brutes, every one of them, brutes or hysterics; but hunters it was *that* day, entertaining some damn fools. Brisk, burned leaves in the air, smell of burning, just dawn; mist on the ground, dawn all green and yellow. We didn't like our *mount,* did we. (*This last to* B.)

B

No.

A

No, I didn't *like* her; she was hysteric *and* a brute.

C

When do I learn to ride? I mean really *ride*.

B

It goes with the marriage.

A

Yes, I didn't trust her; I'd ridden her earlier that fall; she was stupid and cantankerous, shied at a moving shadow. (*To* C.) I said to him, You go on, I'll stay; you go on.

B

Yes.

A

But he looked so hurt I said, Oh, all right, and off we went, into the wood, the green, the gold, the mist knee high to a . . . to your knees! Stupid *cow* of a horse! Couldn't she see the fence in the mist? Did she come on it too fast and shy like that? Over we *went*!

B

Over we *went*.

C

Oh, no!

A

(*To* B.) Could have broken my *neck*, I suppose. Lucky.

B

Well, yes, there *is* that.

A

(*To* B.) We never mounted a hunter again, did we?

B

Nope.

A

Damned cast weighed a ton! And you know what I thought about most?

B

(*Remembering.*) Who he's doing it with; who's he got cornered in what corner, what hallway, who he's poking his little dick into.

A

That he might leave us, that he might decide to get one isn't broken.

C

(*Awe.*) What kind of man *is* this?!

A

(*To* C.) Man-man.

B

(*To* C.) Man-man.

C

How was this happy time? Good times, you said?

B

(*To* C.) Oh, well, we proved we were human. (*To* A.) No?

A

(*To* B.) Of course. (*To* C.) We were fallible. Once you fall—whether you get up or not—once you fall, and they see it, they know you can be pushed. Whether you're made of crockery and smash into pieces, or you're bronze and you clang when you topple, it makes no never mind; it's the plinth is important.

B

(*To* C.) To translate . . .

C

Thank you.

A

(*Sweet smile.*) Thank you.

B

To translate . . . you can go around fixing the *world*, patching everything up—*everyone*—and they're *grate*ful to you—grudgingly, but grateful—but once you fall yourself, prove you're not quite as *much* better than they are than they thought, then they'll *let* you go right on doing everything for them, fixing the world et cetera, but they won't hate you quite so much . . . because you're not perfect.

A

(*Very bright.*) And so everything's *better*. Nice and better. Doesn't that make it a good time? He *doesn't* leave you for something else; he's sweet and gives you a big diamond ring, and you don't have to get back up on a hunter anymore. Doesn't that make it a happy time?

C

Do I get to shoot the horse?

B

(*Laughs.*) I *beg* your pardon?!

A

(*Whoops!*) Whoooo! Never occurred to me!

(A *and* B *laugh together.*)

C

(*Grit.*) I'll never become you—either of you.

B

(*Looks at* C.) Oh, stop! (*To* A.) And the great ring—the big diamond? You don't wear it anymore?

A

(*Suddenly sober.*) Gone.

B

(*Sobered too.*) Oh?

A

I *sold* it.

B

Oh?

A

(*A little bitter.*) I've sold *everything*. Well, not everything . . . but most. Money doesn't go as far these days? Money doesn't go *anywhere*! I have no money. I have *money*, but I eat into it . . . every year; every year it's less.

B

We should cut back; we should . . .

A

Don't talk to me about cutting back! It's all paste! It's fake! All the jewelry sitting in the vault, in the bank? It's all fake!

C

Why is it there? Why do you . . . why do we *bother*?

A

(*Contempt.*) Huh!

B

(*To* C, *then to* A.) Because we take it out and we wear it? Because the fake look as good as the real, even feels the same, and why should anybody know our business? (*Specifically to* A.) No?

C

Appearances?

B

Appearances? That which appears to be?

C

I mean, who are we trying to impress?

A

Ourselves. You'll learn. I took the big diamond in. When we bought it—when he brought it in for me, he said. . . .

B

This is a perfect stone; I've never seen a better one. You ever want to sell this you bring it back to me I'll give you better than you paid for it. He patted my hand. Pat-pat.

A

Pat-pat. And so I took it back—after he died after the cancer and all, after all that. They looked at it; they said it was deeply flawed, or it was cloudy . . . or something.

B

Sons of bitches!

A

They offered me a third of what he paid for it, and the dollar wasn't worth half of what it had been?

C

(*To* A.) Didn't you sue? (*To* B.) I mean, what can we do? We just can't . . .

A

(*Accepting.*) What can you *do*? There's nothing you can *do*. You go *on*; you . . . eat *into* yourself. Starving people absorb their own bodies. The money's there—the investments are there, except less each year; it absorbs itself. It's all you've planned to *count* on *isn't*; the extras?

B

(*To* A.) The big diamond, eh?

A

The big diamond . . . *and* most of the rest. Well, what does it matter? It's all glitter.

C

(*Protest.*) No! It's more than that! It's tangible proof . . . that we're valuable . . . (*embarrassed*) . . . that we're valued.

A
(*Shrugs.*) Well, it's gone; all the glitter's gone.

B
(*Rue.*) Yup. (*Waves.*) Bye.

C
Are there any *other* surprises?

B
(*Grating laugh.*) Oh, yeah; lots!

A
Oh, my dear; you just wait. (*Over toward the bed.*) She hides the money. Whatever she gets for the jewelry she keeps in cash, and spends a little whenever there isn't enough of the regular. There's a lot; she can't spend it all—without people knowing what she's doing, I mean. She hides it, and then eventually she can't remember where she hid it, and she can't find it . . . ever. And she can't tell anybody.

(*Silence.*)

B
(*A little shy.*) Is the cancer bad?

A
When is it good?

C
How bad?

A
(*Mocking.*) Fill me *in*; fill me in! (*To* C.) Pretty terrible! (*To* B; *softer tone.*) Six years; I told you that; it takes him six years from when he knows it—when they tell him he has it—to when he goes. Prostate—spreads to the

bladder, spreads to the bone, spreads to the brain, and to the liver, of course; everything does—the *ancients* knew something. It's all right at first—except for the depression, *and* the fear—it's all right at first, but then the pain comes, slowly, growing, and then the day he screams in the bathroom, and I rush in; I expect to see him lying there, but no, he's standing at the toilet, and his face is filled with horror and he points to the bowl, and I look, and it's all pink in there, that the blood is coming with the urine now. And it's all downhill from there: the pink becomes red, and then there's blood in the bed, at night, as I'm lying with him, holding him; and then there's . . . no! Why go on with it?! (*To* c; *ugly.*) It's terrible! And there's nothing you can do to prepare yourself! I don't like you; you deserve it!

C

(*So softly.*) Thank you.

A

(*Quietly dismissive.*) You're welcome.

C

I don't like you either.

B

(*Pause.*) And so it goes. (*A silence.* a *moves to the bed, sits on it, opposite from him.*)

A

(*Speaks directly to him; now he can hear her, can respond.*) I had a premonition. I know you say there's no such thing, but I *had* one. It was I died. (*His hand up.*) Oh, stop it! You don't think I'm going to? You can hardly—wait! Just you wait! I died, you see, and when I did it—when I died—I was all alone . . . no one there in the room with me—the hospital room: I was back in that awful hospital! (*Suddenly weepy.*) Why didn't you

take me *out* of there?! Why did you leave me in
that . . . (*He tries to touch her, to comfort her.*) Don't you
touch me!! There I was, and I was in a coma, in and
out, in and out. Sometimes I'd wake up and wonder
who I was, and *where* I was, and who were all those
people looking at me? Sometimes I wouldn't wake
up . . . not all the way, and I'd half try, and then I
wouldn't. You brought me flowers, you brought freesia.
You know I love freesia; that's why you bring them to
me, because I *love* them! Why do you do that?! You
hate me; why do you do that?! What do you want?! You
want something. Well, you just wait. You'll get what's
coming to you. In my premonition I knew I was dead,
and it didn't seem to matter any, and I was all alone.
There was no one there with me and I was *dead*! No
one! Just the chauffeur and the maid. I was there an
hour, and I was *dead*, and then *you* came in, and you
had your flowers, your freesia. You came into the room,
and they were there, and I was dead, and you stopped
at the door of the room, and you knew right away, and
you stopped and you . . . *thought*! (*Loathing.*) I *watched*
you *think*! And your face didn't change. (*Wistful.*) Why
didn't your face ever change? And there you were, and
you thought, and you decided, and you walked over to
the bed, and you touched my hand, and you bent
down, and you kissed me on the forehead . . . for them!
They were there and they were watching and you kissed
me for *them*! (*Softer.*) And then you stood up, still holding on to my hand, as if . . . what? You didn't know
what to do with it? You held on to my hand, and my
hand wasn't warm anymore, was it? My hand was cold,
wasn't it? (*Pause.*) *Wasn't* it?

(*He looks at her once more, shudders, weeps, looks back at
"*A.*" A *moves away from the bed.*)

B

(*Softly.*) And so it goes.

C

(*To* A; *slowly, with great emphasis, but no anger.*) I . . . will
. . . not . . . become . . . you. I will *not.* I . . . I deny
you.

A

(*Mildly amused.*) Oh? Yes? You *deny* me? (*To them all.*)
Yes? You all deny me? (*To* C.) You deny me? (*To* B.) I
suppose you do too. (B *lowers her gaze.*) Yes; of course.
(*To him.*) And, of course, *you* deny me. (*He looks at her.*)
(*General.*) Well, that's all right: I deny you too; I deny
you all. (*To* C.) I deny *you,* (*to* B) and I deny *you,* (*to
him*) and, of course, I deny *you.* (*General.*) I'm *here,* and
I deny you *all;* I deny every *one* of you.

C

Is it like this? What about the happy times . . . the
happiest moments? *I haven't* had them yet, have I? All
done at twenty-six? I can't imagine that. I had *some,* of
course, some of what probably will *be* the happiest even
when I get to the point I can begin to think about
looking back without feeling silly, though God knows
when *that* will be!—not feeling silly—if *ever.* Confir-
mation, for example, that wonderful time: the white
dress Mother made, Sis all jealous and excited, jumping up and down and sulking at the same time. But
even now, you see, I'm remembering, and what I'm
remembering doesn't have to do with what I *felt,* but
what I remember. They say you can't remember pain.
Well, maybe you can't remember pleasure, either—in
the same way, I mean, in the way you can't remember
pain. Maybe all you can remember is the memory of
it . . . remembering, remembering it. I *know* my best
times—what is it? happiest?—haven't happened yet.
They're to *come.* Aren't they? Please? And . . . and whatever evil comes, whatever loss and taking away comes,
won't it all be balanced out? Please? I'm not a fool, but
there *is* a lot of happiness along the way. *Isn't* there?!

And isn't it always ahead? Aren't I *right*? Aren't I? I
mean . . . all along the way? No? Please?

B

(*Comes downstage to where* C *is not—either right or left, leaving center free for* A *later. Shakes her head to* C, *not unkindly.*)
Silly, silly girl; silly baby. The happiest time? Now;
now . . . always. This must be the happiest time: half
of being adult done, the rest ahead of me. Old enough
to be a *little* wise, past being *really* dumb . . . (*An aside
to* C.) No offense.

C

(*Looking forward: tight smile.*) None taken.

B

Enough shit gone through to have a sense of the shit
that's ahead, but way past sitting and *playing* in it. This
has to be the happiest time—in theory, anyway. Things
nibble away, of course; your job is to know *that*, too.
The wood *may* be rotten under your feet—your nicely
spread legs—and you'll be up to your ass in sawdust
and dry rot before you know it, before you know it,
before you can say, This is the happiest time. Well, I
can *live* with that, *die* with that. I mean, these things
happen, but what I like most about being where I
am—and fifty *is* a peak, in the sense of a mountain.

C

(*An aside.*) Fifty-two.

B

Yes, I know, thank you. What I like most about being
where I am is that there's a lot I don't have to go
through anymore, and that doesn't mean closing
down—for *me*, at any rate. It opens up whole vistas—
of decline, of obsolescence, peculiarity, but really
interesting! Standing up here right on top of the middle

of it *has* to be the happiest time. I mean, it's the only
time you get a three-hundred-and-sixty-degree view—
see in all directions. Wow! What a view!

(A *moves downstage center,* B *and* C *stay where they are.*)

A

(*Shakes her head; chuckles; to* B *and* C.) You're both such
children. The happiest moment of all? Really? The
happiest moment? (*To the audience now.*) Coming to the
end of it, I think, when all the waves cause the greatest
woes to subside, leaving breathing space, time to con-
centrate on the greatest woe of all—that blessed
one—the end of it. Going through the whole thing
and coming out . . . not out *beyond* it, of course, but sort
of to . . . one side. None of that "further shore" non-
sense, but to the point where you *can* think about yourself in the third person without being crazy. I've waked
up in the morning, and I've thought, well, now, she's
waking up, and now she's going to see what works—
the eyes, for example. Can she *see*? She *can*? Well,
good, I suppose; so much for that. Now she's going to
test all the other stuff—the joints, the inside of the
mouth, and now she's going to have to pee. What's she
going to do—go for the walker? Lurch from chair to
chair—pillar to post? Is she going to call for somebody—anybody . . . the tiniest thought there might be
nobody there, that she's not making a sound, that
maybe she's not alive—so's anybody'd notice, that is?
I can do that. I can think about myself that way, which
means, I suppose, that that's the way I'm *living*—beside
myself, to one side. Is that what they mean by that?—
I'm beside myself? I don't think so. I think they're talking about *another* kind of joy. There's a difference between knowing you're going to *die* and *knowing* you're
going to die. The second is better; it moves away from
the theoretical. I'm rambling, aren't I?

B

(*Gently; face forward.*) A little.

A

(*To* B.) Well, we *do* that at ninety, or whatever I'm supposed to be. I mean, give a girl a break! (*To the audience again now.*) Sometimes when I wake up and start thinking about myself like that—like I was watching—I really get the feeling that I *am dead*, but going on at the same time, and I wonder if she can talk and fear and . . . and then I wonder which has died—me, or the one I think about. It's a fairly confusing business. I'm rambling. (*A gesture to stop* B.) Yes; I know! (*To the audience.*) I was talking about . . . what: coming to the end of it, yes. So. There it is. You asked after all. That's the happiest moment. (A *looks to* C *and* B, *puts her hand out, takes theirs.*) When it's all done. When we stop. When we can stop.

END

℗ PLUME

GREAT THEATER

☐ **M. BUTTERFLY by David Henry Hwang. With an Afterword by the play-wright.** 1988 Tony Award-Winner for Best Play and now a major motion picture from Warner Bros. "A many-splendored theatrical treasure. A thrilling drama. A sensational real-life story of love and treachery."—Frederick Winship, *United Press International* (272599—$9.00)

☐ **THE KENTUCKY CYCLE by Robert Schenkkan.** In this series of nine short plays, Pulitzer Prize-winning playwright Robert Schenkkan has created a mesmerizing epic saga of rural Kentucky—an unblinking look at the truth behind our American mythology, and at the men and women who founded this country. "Aspires to nothing less than the history of the U.S. . . . strives for mythic power—and attains it."—*Time* (269679—$14.00)

☐ **THE DESTINY OF ME A Play by Larry Kramer author of *The Normal Heart*.** Funny, gutsy, and unabashedly emotional . . . has the power to hit us where it hurts—in the heart. AIDS activist Ned Weeks, frightened of dying of the disease . . . checks himself into an experimental treatment program run by the very doctor that his militant organization has been criticizing most. "Overwhelmingly powerful."—Frank Rich, *The New York Times* (270162—$9.95)

☐ **JEFFREY by Paul Rudnick.** "The hottest ticket off-Broadway . . . Even with AIDS lurking in the background, *Jeffrey* sparkles. Mr. Rudnick . . . has come up with some of the funniest lines and deftest gimmicks onstage today. [He] is a master of one-liners."—*Wall Street Journal* (271207—$7.95)

☐ **LATER LIFE *And Two Other Plays*: The Old Boy *and* The Snow Ball. by A.R. Gurney.** This collection of three plays brings us incomparable Gurney—mature, masterful, and hilarious. All three works skillfully juxtapose conflicting emotions to blend wit and sadness, self-realization with self-delusion, and bar-ren interior lives with the façade of prosperous middle-class existences. "There's no dramatist like him on either side of the Atlantic."—*The New Yorker* (272513—$10.95)

Prices slightly higher in Canada.